THE DALAI LAMA'S
LITTLE BOOK OF BUDDHISM

THE DALAI LAMA'S LITTLE BOOK OF BUDDHISM

HIS HOLINESS THE DALAI LAMA

Foreword by Robert Thurman

HAMPTON ROADS

Cover design by Jim Warner
Cover photo © 360b / ShutterStock
Interior designed by Kathryn Sky-Peck

This revised edition published in 2015 by
Hampton Roads Publishing Company, Inc.
Charlottesville, VA 22906
Distributed by Red Wheel/Weiser, LLC
www.redwheelweiser.com
ISBN: 978-1-57174-729-7

Library of Congress Cataloging-in-Publication Data available upon request

Printed on acid-free paper in Canada
FR

10 9 8 7 6 5 4

Contents

FOREWORD

I am honored to write a "little introduction" to His
Holiness the Dalai Lama's *Little Book of Buddhism*! In
an age when the internet is trolled in a misguided search
for "truths," one can find many quotes there attributed to
His Holiness; many of these quotes are things that I am
sure he did not say, though usually the misattributions are
well-meaning, if not a bit cloying and over-sentimental.
How lucky we are to have this current volume, directly
authored by His Holiness. This *Little Book* is so encour-
aging and precious—His Holiness' patient and gentle but
highly acute intelligence and unfailingly honest and direct

expression come shining through. All of the short aphorisms are well chosen by the formidable compiler and editor, Ms. Renuka Singh, who has known His Holiness and worked on many Buddhist projects over the years. Her deep experience of the subject is well demonstrated by her excellent selections for this collection.

The other day a good friend of mine complained to someone else in a conversation I was part of, "Tell me—isn't the Dalai Lama *ever* wrong?"

The other person remained silent, though he was clearly trying to think of something to fault, just to show he wasn't idealizing the man. In an effort to help out, I intervened, "Well, I think he *is* wrong sometimes!"

My friend looked excited.

I said, "I think he is *too* nice sometimes, always polite

and gentle, not wanting to push people beyond what he thinks they can absorb, so he can be over-solicitous of people."

My friend was a bit disappointed.

The thing about such reactions to the Dalai Lama's remarkably no-nonsense persona is that it resembles the reaction most modern people have to the Shakya-muni Buddha as a figure in history. Scholars about "Bud-dhism" are, surprisingly, mostly like that, as are also "ordinary" people; they just cannot grasp that there might be such a thing as an "enlightened person." They are so full of misplaced confidence in the absolute right-ness of the way they see things that they cannot imagine a consciousness higher and more perceptive than their own—actually enlightened.

"Enlightened" in this sense doesn't just mean "rational," which is how we have tended to think due to our definition of the Western "Enlightenment" of the 17th and 18th centuries, also known as the "Age of Reason." A buddha's enlightenment is believed indeed to make him what is called "personification of reason" (Sanskrit, *pramābhūta*), but his enlightenment also makes him universally compassionate, blissful, and loving, to an almost divine degree. Buddha is called "the God beyond gods" (*Devātideva*), and the "God who Lovingly Looks After Us" (*Avalokiteshvara*)—a buddha who remains a bodhisattva (buddha-to-be) forever in order to remain close to and helpful to suffering beings.

In Tibetan belief, the Dalai Lama is believed to be an important manifestation of Avalokiteshvara's myriad emanations who range around the planet among all species of beings in order to alleviate suffering and benefit those in need of help.

I myself do not know for sure if the Dalai Lama really is such an emanation; I don't even know for sure if there is any such thing as a perfectly enlightened buddha, as briefly sketched above. I would have to be enlightened myself in order to know that for sure— and I am not. And in the fifty years during which I have personally known the Dalai Lama, I have often heard him disclaim any such status for himself, and even contradict others who pronounce him something extraordinary. I introduced him at his first lecture in Saunders Theater at Harvard in 1981, and I went into detail about him being the incarnation of Avalokiteshvara, and explained who Avalokiteshvara of the thousand arms and eyes is, etc. etc., and as he was rising to go to the podium to speak, he whispered to me, with a mixture of a twinkle and a frown, something to the effect, "Don't over-promise for your speaker in case he might disgrace you!" I certainly blushed as I sat down—it embarrasses me to remember it—but he certainly did give a marvelous address, entirely off the cuff, in broken but heartfelt and expressive English, with some help from his interpreter.

However, in spite of his protests, he is an amazing person. As I get older, both he and the Shakyamuni Buddha appear to me to be more and more amazing—as I watch him in action, it seems at moments as if they are the very same person. I don't know, but at least, what

I have learned of their deeds, and experienced of His Holiness personally, has gradually convinced me that there *is* such a thing as a higher consciousness. There are people who see more clearly than I do, than most people do. They do have good advice, which can help us again and again as we come back to it again and again and apply it to the ongoing struggles of life. And that means that we also, in success and adversity, in calm and upset moments, can learn step by step to deal with our own unruly emotions, and then get along better with others. We can learn to understand their sometimes surprising and often troubling behaviors, and so "uplevel" our dealings with them, and not get dragged into vicious cycles of reactivity. Quoting at random from this *Little Book*:

"Sometimes your dear friend, though still the same person, feels more like an enemy. Instead of love, you feel hostility. But with genuine love and compassion, another person's appearance or behavior has no effect on your attitude."

This kind of thing certainly does happen, even in families. And here, the Dalai Lama is honoring us: he is implying that we also can attain such a genuine love and compassion. He thus encourages us to make the effort, since such an expanded emotional security is indeed attainable by us, too, slowly but surely. He couldn't say such a thing if (a) he himself hadn't made such a progress in freeing himself from the "normal" kind of hostile reactivity under stress, and (b) hadn't seen people around him also shift in that direction.

This is movement toward "enlightenment," this kind of inner strength and cheerful demeanor from the heart. It is not at all a matter of meditating alone and having a *eureka!* moment, and then ascending away from everyone into some imagined state of self-centered, frozen isolation.

So Buddha might have been wrong, the Dalai Lama might be wrong. Actually they both encourage us to try to find out where they do go wrong. The Dalai Lama often likes to quote a famous verse from the *Dense Array Sutra*: "Mendicants! Wise persons take my words as a goldsmith buys his gold, after cutting, melting, and rubbing on a touchstone, and only after thorough examination do they accept them—not just out of devotion." Recently I was present at a 10,000 person teaching in

Switzerland where His Holiness was commenting on this verse, and at one point he leaned passionately forward in the high teacher's seat (the traditional Tibetan formal setup), and said, "You must think carefully about what I am saying, not just listen passively. Why, I can just see in my mind's eye Shakyamuni Buddha himself, begging his disciples, 'Please find out if I said something wrong! Please think this over and look for faults and advantages and then make use of it, make it your own.'" Then he quoted the verse, and his posture completely sent out the message that the teacher is the servant of the student, seeking to provide the students the tools with which to improve and liberate themselves; that the teacher is not just a domineering authority figure who thinks he has something his students don't and their only hope is just to obey and imitate him as best they can. It was deeply moving, but I could sense a slight discomfort on the part of those other teachers in the audience who were thinking they are the authorities, and those students who were expecting the teacher to do something for them that they wouldn't have to do for themselves.

So here we are with the great and deep, sweet and challenging, supporting and inspiring aphorisms of this wonderful person offering us his invaluable service, providing us with tools of insights he has gained from eight decades of his broad and often difficult experience, and his vast and persistent studies of the thoughts of others in the Buddhist spiritual university tradition, and of his own thinking patterns in the meditational university of his mind. They are so well arranged by the sensitive and learned editor, I welcome you to them in the fullest confidence that you will find these gems of advice enlightening to both head and heart. Whatever you may think about yourself, you must have an excellent intelligence or you wouldn't have opened this book. Your good heart will find here nourishment, skill and courage to proceed, step by step. Finally, again at random,

> "Cultivating closeness and warmth for others automatically puts the mind at ease. It is the ultimate source of success in life."

—Robert A. F. "Tenzin Dharmakīrti" Thurman, Professor of Buddhist Studies, Columbia University

INTRODUCTION

We are the creators of our own happiness and suffering, for everything originates in the mind. So we need to take responsibility for whatever, good or bad, we experience.

This book contains the essence of Buddhism and offers practical wisdom for our daily lives in the words of His Holiness the Dalai Lama. His inspiring thoughts help to improve our state of mind, and to discover deep peace within.

This chain of Buddhist thoughts consists of pithy reflections on our need to rid ourselves of the preoccupation with mundane concerns to find refuge in

Buddha, Dharma, and Sangha. It teaches us the law of karma, where, by living according to the Ten Virtuous Actions and the Four Noble Truths, we can achieve the free heart of a Bodhisattva.

—Renuka Singh

THE DALAI LAMA'S
LITTLE BOOK
OF BUDDHISM

The common enemy of all religious disciplines is selfishness of mind. For it is just this which causes ignorance, anger and passion, which are at the root of all the troubles of the world.

Buddha is the teacher, Dharma is the actual refuge and the Sangha is the one which assists in understanding or establishing the objects of refuge.

When we take the Buddha as an authority, as a reliable teacher, we do so on the basis of having investigated and examined his principal teaching—the Four Noble Truths.

Whenever Buddhism has taken root in a new land, there has been a certain variation in the style in which it is observed. The Buddha himself taught differently according to the place, the occasion and the situation of those who were listening to him.

All of us have a great responsibility to take the essence of Buddhism and put it into practice in our own lives.

Buddhahood is a state free of all obstructions to knowledge and disturbing emotions. It is the state in which the mind is fully evolved.

From the earliest stages of our growth, we are completely dependent upon our mother's care and it is very important for us that she express her love. If children do not receive proper affection, in later life they will often find it hard to love others.

Samsara, our conditioned existence in the perpetual cycle of habitual tendencies, and nirvana, genuine freedom from such an existence, are nothing but different manifestations of a basic continuum. So this continuity of consciousness is always present.

This is the meaning of tantra.

Through actual practice in his daily life, man well fulfils the aim of all religion, whatever his denomination.

We can speak of an effect and a cause on the disturbing side as well as on the liberating side.

According to Buddhist practice, there are three states or steps. The initial stage is to reduce attachment towards life. The second stage is the elimination of desire and attachment to this samsara. Then in the third stage, self-cherishing is eliminated.

The three stages—birth, death and the intermediate state—are also established in terms of the subtlety of their levels of consciousness. Upon the basis of the continuity of the stream of consciousness is established the existence of rebirth and reincarnation.

Encountering sufferings will definitely contribute to the elevation of your spiritual practice, provided you are able to transform the calamity and misfortune into the path.

Faith dispels doubt and hesitation, it liberates you from suffering and delivers you to the city of peace and happiness.

If subconscious anger had a parallel in Buddhist writings, it would have to do with what is called mental unhappiness or dissatisfaction. This is regarded as the source of anger and hostility. We can see subconscious anger in terms of a lack of awareness, as well as an active misconstruing of reality.

Guilt is incompatible with our thinking as you are part of an action but not fully responsible for it. You are just part of the contributing factor. However, in some cases one must repent, deliberately claim responsibility, have regret, and never commit the mistake again.

In the beginning of Buddhist practice, our ability to serve others is limited. The emphasis is on healing ourselves, transforming our minds and hearts. But as we continue, we become stronger and increasingly able to serve others.

Firstly, we should re-examine our own attitude towards others and constantly check ourselves to see whether we are practicing properly. Before pointing our finger at others we should point it towards ourselves. Secondly, we must be prepared to admit our faults and stand corrected.

Suffering increases your inner strength. Also, wishing for suffering makes the suffering disappear.

Even when we are helping others and are engaged in charity work, we should not regard ourselves in a very haughty way as great protectors benefitting the weak.

An area in Tibetan Buddhism which may be of interest to scientists is the relationship between the physical elements and the nerves, in particular the relationship between the elements in the brain and consciousness. This involves changes in consciousness, happy or unhappy states of mind, the effect they have on the elements within the brain, and the consequent effect that this has on the body.

According to its level of subtlety, consciousness is classified into three levels: the waking state or gross level of consciousness; the consciousness of the dream state which is more subtle; and the consciousness during sleep, dreamless sleep, which is subtler still.

The metaphor of light is a common image in all the major religious traditions. In the Buddhist context, light is particularly associated with wisdom and knowledge; darkness is associated with ignorance and a state of mis-knowledge.

In yoga tantra, the highest dimension of Buddhist practice, there is no distinction between gender. In this final life in which you attain Buddhahood, there is no difference whether you are male or female.

The creatures that inhabit this earth—be they human beings or animals—are here to contribute, each in its own particular way, to the beauty and prosperity of the world.

The Buddhist notion of attachment is not what people in the West assume. We say that the love of a mother for her only child is free of attachment.

We are born and reborn countless number of times, and it is possible that each being has been our parent at one time or another. Therefore, it is likely that all beings in this universe have familial connections.

The process of dying begins with the dissolution of the elements within the body. It has eight stages, beginning with the dissolution of the earth element, then the water, fire, and wind elements. The next four stages are visions in terms of color: appearance of a white vision, increase of the red element, black near-attainment, and finally the clear light of death.

Do your best and do it according to your own inner standard—call it conscience—not just according to society's knowledge and judgement of your deeds.

For discovering one's true inner nature, I think one should try to take some time, with quiet and relaxation, to think more inwardly and to investigate the inner world.

When one is very involved in hatred or attachment, if there is time or possibility during that very
moment, just try to look inward and ask: "What is
attachment? What is the nature of anger?"

To develop genuine devotion, you must know the meaning of teachings. The main emphasis in Buddhism is to transform the mind, and this transformation depends upon meditation. In order to meditate correctly, you must have knowledge.

Three qualities enable people to understand the teachings: objectivity, which means an open mind; intelligence, which is the critical faculty to discern the real meaning by checking the teachings of Buddha; and interest and commitment, which means enthusiasm.

Anything that contradicts experience and logic should be abandoned.

It is through listening that your mind will turn with faith and devotion, and you will be able to cultivate joy within your mind and make your mind stable.

Mahayana has four reliances.

First: reliance on the teaching, not on the teacher.

Second: reliance on the meaning, not on the words that express it.

Third: reliance on the definitive meaning, not on the provisional meaning.

Fourth: reliance on the transcendent wisdom of deep experience, not on mere knowledge.

If we see pride among people who have no idea about Dharma, it is understandable. However, if afflictive emotions and haughtiness are present among Dharma practitioners, it is a great disgrace to the practice.

Individuals who are best suited for practice of Dharma are those who are not only intellectually gifted, but also have single-minded faith and dedication and are wise.

Although individuals may be highly intelligent, they are sometimes dogged by skepticism and doubts. They are clever, but they tend to be hesitant and skeptical and are never really able to settle down. These people are the least receptive.

As a spiritual trainee, you must be prepared to endure the hardships involved in a genuine spiritual pursuit and be determined to sustain your effort and will. You must anticipate the multiple obstacles that you are bound to encounter along the path and understand the key to successful practice is never to lose your determination.

The story of the Buddha's personal life is the story of someone who attained full enlightenment through hard work and unwavering dedication.

Laziness will stop your progress in your spiritual practice.

When a day seems to be long, idle gossip makes our day seem shorter. But it is one of the worst ways in which we waste our time. If a tailor just holds the needle in his hand and goes on talking to a customer, the tailoring does not get finished. Besides, the needle might prick his finger. In short, meaningless gossip prevents us from doing any kind of work.

If you rely on someone who has lower qualities than yourself, that will lead to your degeneration. If you rely on someone who has qualities similar to yourself, you will stay where you are. It is only if you rely on someone who has better qualities than yourself, that you will achieve sublime status.

The advantage of relying on a spiritual teacher is that if you have accumulated an action that would project you into a negative state of existence, the result of that could be experienced just in this life in the form of minor sufferings or minor problems, or even experiencing the result in a dream and through that way one could destroy the destructive results of negative actions.

If you go more deeply into your own spiritual practice, emphasizing wisdom and compassion, you will encounter the suffering of other sentient beings again and again, and you will have the capacity to acknowledge it, respond to it and feel deep compassion rather than apathy or impotence.

When contemplating suffering, do not fall into the feeling of self-importance or conceit. Cultivating wisdom helps us to avoid these pitfalls. But it is hard to generalize because each person's courage and forbearance are unique.

The more we care for the happiness of others, the greater is our own sense of well-being.

A single word or expression in tantra can have four different meanings corresponding to the four levels of interpretation. These levels are known as the four modes of understanding. They are:

i) the literal meaning;

ii) the general meaning;

iii) the hidden meaning; and

iv) the ultimate meaning.

Calm abiding is a heightened state of awareness when your body and mind become especially flexible, receptive and serviceable. Special insight is also a heightened state of awareness, in which your faculty of analysis is immensely advanced. Thus calm abiding is absorptive in nature, whereas special insight is analytic in nature.

There is a true feminist movement in Buddhism. Following her attainment of bodhicitta, the goddess Tara looked upon those striving towards full awakening and she felt that there were too few women who attained Buddhahood. So she vowed, "I have developed bodhicitta as a woman. For all of my lifetimes along the path I vow to be born as a woman, and in my final lifetime when I attain Buddhahood, then too I will be a woman."

The problems we encounter are never the result of starting a project or work on an inappropriate day or time. Buddha always talked about negative experiences as the result of having performed negative actions. So, for a good practitioner there is no good day or bad day.

There is no way to escape death, it is just like trying to escape when you are surrounded by four great mountains touching the sky. There is no escape from these four mountains of birth, old age, sickness, and death.

Ageing destroys youth, sickness destroys health, degeneration of life destroys all excellent qualities, and death destroys life. Even if you are a great runner, you cannot run away from death. You cannot stop death with your wealth, through your magic performances, or recitation of mantras or even medicines. Therefore, it is wise to prepare for your death.

Discipline is a supreme ornament and, whether worn by old, young or middle-aged, it gives birth only to happiness. It is perfume *par excellence* and, unlike ordinary perfumes which travel only with the wind, its refreshing aroma travels spontaneously in all directions. A peerless ointment, it brings relief from the hot pains of delusion.

Due to karmic influences, the world appears in different ways to different people. When a human being, a god, and a *preta*—three sentient beings—look at one bowl of water, the karmic factors make the human being see it as water, while the god sees nectar, and the *preta* sees blood.

A blossoming tree becomes bare and stripped in autumn. Beauty changes into ugliness, youth into old age, and fault into virtue. Things do not remain the same and nothing really exists. Thus, appearances and emptiness exist simultaneously.

Some people who are sweet and attractive, strong and healthy, happen to die young. They are masters in disguise teaching us about impermanence.

Natural environment sustains the life of all beings universally. Trees are referred to in accounts of the principal events of Buddha's life. His mother leaned against a tree for support as she gave birth to him. He attained enlightenment seated beneath a tree, and finally passed away as trees stood witness overhead.

The Bible says that swords can be turned into plough-shares. It is a beautiful image, a weapon transformed into a tool to serve basic human needs, representing an attitude of inner and outer disarmament.

The true sufferings and true causes of sufferings are the effect and cause on the side of things that we do not want; the true cessation and the true paths are the effect and cause on the side of things that we desire.

The truth of suffering is that we experience many different types of suffering: things such as headaches; suffering of changes; feeling of restlessness after being comfortable; and all-pervasive suffering that acts as the basis of the first two categories and is under the control of karma and the disturbing mind.

From one point of view we can say that we have human bodies and are practicing the Buddha's teachings and are thus much better than insects. But we can also say that insects are innocent and free from guile, whereas we often lie and misrepresent ourselves in devious ways in order to achieve our ends or better ourselves. From this perspective, we are much worse than insects.

No matter who we ate with, we often think things like, "I am stronger than he," "I am more beautiful than she," "I am more intelligent," and so forth— we generate much pride. This is not good. Instead, we should always remain humble.

To develop patience, you need someone who wilfully hurts you. Such people give us the real opportunity to practice tolerance. They test our inner strength in a way that even our guru cannot. Basically, patience protects us from being discouraged.

It is better not to avoid events or persons who annoy you and give rise to anger, if your anger is not too strong. But if the encounter is not possible, work on your anger and develop compassion by yourself.

The three physical non-virtues are killing, stealing, and sexual misconduct. The four verbal non-virtues are lying, divisiveness, harsh speech, and senseless speech. The three mental non-virtues are covetousness, harmful intent, and wrong view.

We find that between the past and the future there is an extremely thin line—something that cannot really withstand analysis. Past and future exist in relation to the present. But if the present cannot be posited, how can past and future be posited? This is a demonstration of dependent origination.

We learn from the principle of dependent origination that things and events do not come into being without causes. Suffering and unsatisfactory conditions are caused by our own delusions and the contaminated actions induced by them.

For a bodhisattva to be successful in accomplishing the practice of the six perfections—generosity, ethical discipline, tolerance, joyous effort, concentration, and wisdom—cooperation with fellow beings and kindness towards them are extremely important.

Suffering originates from various causes and conditions. But the root cause of our pain and suffering lies in our own ignorant and undisciplined state of mind. The happiness we seek can be attained only through the purification of our minds.

The criterion that distinguishes a school as Buddhist is its acceptance of four fundamental tenets, known as the four seals:

i) All composite phenomena are impermanent.

ii) All contaminated things and events are unsatisfactory.

iii) All phenomena are empty and selfless.

iv) Nirvana is true peace.

Vegetarianism is very admirable. However, according to Buddhism, there is no unequivocal prohibition against eating meat. What is specifically prohibited is taking any meat that you have ordered with the knowledge, or even the suspicion, that it has been killed especially for you.

Try to consider as transitory all adverse circumstances and disturbances. Like ripples in a pool, they occur and soon disappear.

Our lives are conditioned by karma. They are characterized by endless cycles of problems. One problem appears and passes, and soon another one begins.

The essence of all spiritual life is your attitude towards others. Once you have pure and sincere motives all the rest follows.

You can develop the right attitude toward others if you have kindness, love and respect for them, and a clear realization of the oneness of all human beings.

It is faith that removes mental turbidity and makes your mind clear.

Guilt is something that can be overcome. It does not exist in Buddhist terminology. With the Buddha nature, all negative things can be purified.

In one sense, we can say it is delusion—in the form of the wisdom derived from delusions—that actually destroys itself.

Similarly, it is the blissful experience of emptiness induced by sexual desire that dissolves the force of sexual impulses.

Irrespective of whether we are believers or agnostics, whether we believe in God or karma, everyone can pursue moral ethics.

Real compassion comes from seeing the suffering of others. You feel a sense of responsibility, and you want to do something for them.

Sometimes your dear friend, though still the same person, feels more like an enemy. Instead of love, you feel hostility. But with genuine love and compassion, another person's appearance or behavior has no effect on your attitude.

Ordinary compassion and love give rise to a feeling of closeness, but this is essentially attachment. As long as the other person appears to you as beautiful or good, love remains, but as soon as he or she appears to you as less beautiful or good, your love changes completely.

The teachings of Lord Buddha comprise three graded categories for disciplining the mind—

Shila: training in higher conduct

Samadhi: training in higher meditation, and

Prajna: training in higher wisdom.

Speech and bodily activities which accompany mental processes must not be allowed to run on in unbridled and random ways. Just as a trainer disciplines and calms a wild and wilful steed by rigorous and prolonged training, so must the indiscreet and wandering activities of body and speech be tamed to make them docile, righteous, and skilful.

The healing power of the spirit naturally follows the path of the spirit. It abides not in the stone of fine buildings, nor in the gold of images, nor in the silk from which robes are fashioned, nor even in the paper of holy writ, but it abides in the ineffable substance of the mind and the heart of man. We should sublimate our heart's instinct and purify our thoughts.

I am talking to you and you are listening to me. We are generally under the impression that there is a speaker and an audience and there is the sound of words being spoken. But if I search within myself, I will not find the words, and if you search yourselves you will not find them either—they are all void like empty space. Yet they are not completely nonexistent. This paradox relates to the dual nature of truth.

Many creatures have toiled singly or jointly to make our lives comfortable. The food we eat and the clothes we wear have not just dropped from the sky. Many creatures have laboured to produce them. That is why we should be grateful to all our fellow creatures.

Compassion and loving kindness are the hallmarks

of achievement and happiness.

If one feels very profound compassion, this implies

an intimate connection with another person exists

already.

It is said in our scriptures that we are to cultivate love just like that of a mother towards her only child.

There are many female concerns in the highest yoga tantra. For example, one of the root evils for a man is to abuse or to look down upon a woman. If a man does that, his downfall is inevitable. There is no mention of a comparable downfall for a woman who looks down on a man. So we men are jealous.

Look at one person who annoys you, and use the opportunity to counter your own anger and cultivate compassion. But if the annoyance is too powerful—if you find the person so repulsive that you cannot bear to be in his or her presence—it may be better to look for the exit!

Faith reduces your pride and is the root of veneration. With faith, you can easily traverse from one stage of the spiritual path to another.

Spiritual intimacy is necessary for a practitioner of Buddhism, especially when one is trying to overcome his mental problems.

When you open yourself up mentally, you do so only with someone you trust from the bottom of your heart, someone you feel very close to. To open yourself up in this way is an important step in overcoming mental problems.

The wood-born insects consume the very wood from which they are born. Such utilization of the path to enlightenment is a unique feature of tantra.

In the special dream state, the special dream body is created from the mind and from vital energy within the body. This special dream body is able to dissociate entirely from the gross physical body and travel elsewhere. One way of developing this special dream body is first of all to recognize the dream as a dream when it is over. Then, you find that the dream is malleable, and you can make efforts to gain control over it.

In addition to practicing Buddhism in the waking state, if you can also use your consciousness during sleep for wholesome purposes, then the power of your spiritual practice will be all the greater. Otherwise the few hours of sleep each night will be just a waste.

The *Sutrayana* method is to cultivate a wholesome

mental state when you are going to sleep.

When the clear light nature of the mind is veiled or inhibited from expressing its true essence by the conditioning of afflictive emotions and thoughts, one is said to be caught in *samsara*, the cycle of existence. But when by applying appropriate meditative techniques and practices, one is able to fully experience this state of mind, he or she is on the way to true liberation and full enlightenment.

When a wrong deed has been done, then after learning that it was wrong, one can disclose the deed—in the presence of actual or imagined holy beings—and resolve not to do that action again in the future. This diminishes the force of the ill deed.

Determination, courage, and self-confidence are the key factors for success. If we have firm determination, we can work out obstacles and difficulties. Whatever the circumstances, we should remain humble, modest, and without pride.

When you create the spiritual space and atmosphere that you are seeking through rituals and formalities, then the process will have a powerful effect on your experience. When you lack the inner dimension for that spiritual experience you are aspiring to, then rituals become mere external formalities and just a good excuse for passing time.

Blessings by themselves are not enough. They must come from within. Without your own effort, it is impossible for them to come.

There are two aspects of the path: the method aspect, which includes such practices as compassion and tolerance; and the wisdom or knowledge aspect, which involves the insight to penetrate the nature of reality. It is the latter aspect of the path that is the true antidote to dispelling ignorance.

Certain physical illnesses improve or worsen according to the state of mind.

It would be much more constructive if people tried to understand their supposed enemies.

Learning to forgive is infinitely more useful than merely picking up a stone and throwing it at the object of one's anger, especially when the provocation is extreme.

The grosser consciousness depends heavily on particles of matter. The subtler consciousness is more independent—it does not depend so much on the brain. In the Buddha state, the grosser mind completely disappears. Luminance, radiance, imminence—the three states of subtle mind—disappear in the clear light of the innermost consciousness.

What is reborn are our habits. Enlightenment is the ending of rebirth, which means complete non-attachment or non-identification with all thought, feeling, perception, physical sensations, and ideas.

The observation that good people suffer and evil people enjoy success and recognition is short-sighted. Also this conclusion might have been drawn in haste. If one analyses carefully, one finds that troublemakers are definitely not happy. It is better to behave well, take responsibility for one's actions, and lead a positive life.

The greatest degree of inner tranquility comes from the development of love and compassion.

Cultivating closeness and warmth for others automatically puts the mind at ease. It is the ultimate source of success in life.

True compassion is not just an emotional response but a firm commitment founded on reason. Therefore, a truly compassionate attitude towards others does not change even if they behave negatively.

Through universal altruism, you develop a feeling of responsibility for others and the wish to help them actively overcome their problems.

One should practice spirituality with a motivation similar to that of a child fully absorbed in play. Such a child is so delighted and engrossed in what he is doing that he never feels satisfied or tired. Such should be your mental attitude when practicing Dharma.

If a person has a really deep interest in spiritual growth, he or she cannot do away with the practice of meditation. That is the key to spiritual growth.

Mere prayer or a wish will not affect inner spiritual change. The only way for development is by constant effort through meditation.

In the beginning, practice is not easy. You may encounter difficulties or experience a loss of enthusiasm. Or perhaps there will be too much enthusiasm—then after a few weeks or months, your enthusiasm may wane. You need to develop a constant, persistent approach based on a long-term commitment.

In the quest for mental quiescence, there is a state where striving must be abandoned, for an effortless concentration is necessary. Your mind then becomes very tranquil and achieves a state of wholeness. At that moment, to make an effort would disturb that pure tranquility. So in order to maintain that tranquility, effortless effort must be used.

Such practices as bodhicitta automatically bring calm at the time of death. The mind is then at a very critical period. If you are able to create a strong positive impact at that time, then this becomes a very powerful force in continuing that positive influence in the next life.

We practice various meditations in dream states. The virtue of such practices is that during such states, it is possible to separate the gross levels of consciousness from the gross physical state, and arrive at a subtler level of mind and body.

The teacher is responsible for his or her improper behavior. It is the student's responsibility not to be drawn into it. The blame is on both: the student, because he is too obedient and devoted to the teacher; and the teacher, because he lacks the integrity necessary to be immune to that kind of vulnerability.

If there is love, there is hope that one may have real families, real brotherhood, real equanimity, real peace. If the love within your mind is lost and you see other beings as enemies, then no matter how much knowledge or education or material comfort you have, only suffering and confusion will ensue.

Human beings will continue to deceive and over-power one another. Basically, everyone exists in a state of suffering, so to abuse or mistreat each other is futile. The foundation of all spiritual practice is love. That you practice this well is my only request.

"To do our best" means that at all times in our everyday life we should probe our minds so that we don't feel guilty about our mistakes, even though others don't know about them. If we do that, we are truly doing our best.

One can be deceived by three types of laziness: the laziness of indolence, which is the wish to procrastinate; the laziness of inferiority, which is doubting your capabilities; and the laziness that is attachment to negative actions, or putting great effort into non-virtue.

Listening cultivates wisdom and removes ignorance. It is like a torch that dispels ignorance. If you enrich your mental continuum by listening, no one can steal that wealth. It is the supreme wealth.

Every noble work is bound to encounter problems and obstacles. It is important to check your goal and motivation thoroughly. One should be very truthful, honest, and reasonable. One's action should be good for others, and for oneself as well.

Emptiness should be understood in the context of dependent arising and it should evoke a sense of fullness, of things created by causes and conditions. We should not think that the self is something that was originally there and can be eliminated through meditation. In fact, the self is something that never existed in the first place.

To help others in vast and extensive ways we need to have attained one of the levels of Bodhisattva, that is, to have experienced the direct non-conceptual reality of voidness and to have achieved the power of extra-sensory perception.

Our state of mind plays a major role in our day-to-day experiences as well as in our physical and mental well-being. If a person has a calm and stable mind, this influences his or her attitude and behavior in relation to others. In other words, if someone exists in a peaceful and tranquil state of mind, external surroundings can cause them only a limited disturbance.

It is under the greatest adversity that there exists the greatest potential for doing good, both for oneself and others.

GLOSSARY

Aggregate: Five psycho-physical components that constitute a being such as humans i.e., of form, feelings, recognition, compositional factors and consciousness.

Attachment: It is one of the three poisons of the mind which are attachment, delusion and aversion. If it is taken to an extreme, it becomes insatiable craving, and can also be seen as biased love.

Awareness: It encompasses knowing and being aware of objects and consciousness, and is also viewed as intelligence and knowledge-based state of mind.

Bodhicitta: This is the mind aspiring for enlightenment. It is of two kinds—conventional Bodhicitta and ultimate Bodhicitta. On the conventional or relative level, it is the wish to attain Buddhahood for the sake of all beings, which drives the person to engage in the practice of the path of love, compassion, the six transcendent perfections necessary for achieving that goal. On the absolute level, it is the direct insight into the ultimate nature which is possessed by the Arya Bodhisattvas.

Bodhisattva: A spiritual practitioner who has generated Boddhichitta or the altruistic intention to attain enlightenment for the sake of all living beings. The basic commitment is to work for others and remain purposely within cyclic existence instead of simply seeking freedom from suffering for oneself.

Buddha: The One who is "awakened" or fully enlightened. A fully awakened being achieved the state of perfection having gone through all the trainings on the bodhisattva path and finally realizes one's potential for complete enlightenment, and eliminates all the obscurations to true knowledge and liberation. Their characteristic features are found in the perfection of love, knowledge and power, the attainment of which make one a perfect guide to liberate all beings from miseries.

Buddhahood: This is attainment of a Buddha who has attained total freedom from karmically conditioned existence and the subtle stains which forbids one from achieving omniscience and fully realized or manifested all aspects of Buddha/ body/ speech/ mind/ attributes/ activities.

Consciousness: It refers to a non-material capacity to illuminate and bring to awareness both objective and subjective reality. Consciousness has the quality of luminosity and clarity. There are many types of consciousness such as sensory consciousness and mental consciousness, gross and subtle and so forth.

Cyclic Existence: Life that is conditioned by dissonant mental states and the Karmic imprints characterized by suffering in a cycle of life, death and rebirth, in which the six classes of sentient beings rotate.

Dependent Origination: Or "pratityasamutpada" as known in Sanskrit. It is the most fundamental metaphysical view in Buddhism. This principle asserts that everything exists dependently on other factors. In other words, multiple causes, conditions and factors create things and events. There are three levels of dependent origination: causal dependence, whole's dependence on parts, and mental imputation dependence. This understanding sees the interdependency of self and others, thus cleansing all negative thoughts and emotions and engendering all positive emotions such as compassion. The first level can be understood in greater detail through the twelve links of dependent origination. These comprise: ignorance, motivational tendencies, consciousness, name and form, sensory activity fields, contact, sensation, attachment, grasping, rebirth, birth, aging, and death. All these twelve links are interconnected and each component of the chain contributes to this endless ignorance-filled cycle.

Dharma: The term Dharma means "to hold" or "to maintain." It denotes to teachings or doctrines of the Buddha. After Buddha's enlightenment, Buddha's first sermon was called the First turning the wheel of Dharma. In general it also refers to one's spiritual practice, specifically it refers to the third and the fourth of the Four Noble Truths. The possession of the these two truths protects the individual from suffering as well as the origin of suffering permanently.

Emptiness: This refers to the ultimate nature of reality or the absence of inherent existence and self–identity with reality and all phenomena. The wisdom which realizes this reality frees one from the ignorance of seeing things as independently real, thus setting one free from the chain of miseries. Suchness, actual reality, and ultimate truth are synonymous. Thus, at an internal and external level, all things and events do not possess any independent, intrinsic reality that defines their essence.

Enlightenment: It is the ultimate goal one aspires for on the Buddhist path. One is considered to be enlightened or awakened when one has succeeded in purifying afflictive emotions as well as obstruction to knowledge. A person who has attained enlightenment is called a Buddha or the awakened one.

Equanimity: It is a state of even-mindedness, an unbiased mind toward others. Normally, one's attitude towards other persons is strongly affected by viewing them as friends, enemies or strangers. Hence, one regards others as completely equal and gets rid of partiality towards them. With equanimity you have the same attitude towards friends, enemies and strangers.

Five Inner and Outer Elements: These five elements consist of earth, water, fire, air, and space. They are called the five inner elements that compose our body, whereas the five outer elements refer to the elements that compose our universe.

Four Noble Truths: This is the content of the first discourse given by Sakyamuni Buddha in Sarnath following his attainment of Buddhahood in Bodh Gaya. The four truths are: (a) truth of suffering, (b) the truth of its origins, (c) the truth of its cessation, (d) the truth of the path leading to such cessation. The entire structure of the path to Buddhahood is built on these four truths and thus, the understanding of these Four Noble Truths holds the key to success in one's spiritual practice.

Great Compassion: This is an unconditional love, which is a totally unbiased mind that wishes for the liberation of all sentient beings from suffering and cannot be mistaken for pity which may have a connotation of superiority towards the object of compassion. This is the ground for any practice of the teachings of the Buddha.

Hinayana/Theravada: Buddhist spiritual paths that emphasize individual liberation from the sufferings of cyclic existence, or it is also called the lesser vehicle.

Impermanence: It is one of the marks of causally conditioned phenomena along with suffering and the absence of self-identity. It alludes to the momentary changing nature of things that are always fluid and in flux.

Inherent Existence: Objectively phenomena are viewed to be attributed with an inherent existence in their own right and of themselves. This is to be negated in order to understand the ultimate reality. They are to be identified as independent of any other phenomena such as conception and labelling.

Karma: Karma is the causal factor involved with a dynamic relationship between actions and their results. It is of three kinds: physical, verbal and mental. Karma leaves psychological imprints and tendencies within the mind. Hence, a casual chain is maintained within the mental continuum which can be traced in the present and future lives, and karma ripens as and when it encounters the approximate circumstances and conditions.

Lama: Lama means venerable teacher or guru—someone who is weighty because one is a master of the inner world and is supreme who is unsurpassed. To be a lama, specific qualifications are necessary. These may differ according to the level of spiritual practice.

Liberation: This deals with the freedom from cyclic existence—the cycle of birth, death, and rebirth, and freedom from all forms of physical and mental suffering.

Mahayana: The greater vehicle is known in terms of its motivation, i.e., the practitioner of this path emphasizes altruism and keeps the liberation of all sentient beings as the principal objective.

Mandala: This connotes a circle, wheel, circumference, totality, and assembly of the literary corpus. In a more general usage, this term points to the central and peripheral deities along with the abode described in tantric texts. The mandala generally represents a perfected state of being and perception encompassing all phenomena.

Mantra: It is an abbreviation of two syllables *mana* and *traya,* i.e. mind and protection. So, it can be considered as the protection of the mind from deluded states of existence in order not to inhibit the full expression of Buddha nature. Mantra also refers to the pure sound which is the perfected speech of an enlightened being.

Meditation: It means that one cultivates familiarity with chosen object, be it external or internal, through disciplined mental process. There are two main types of meditation, the calm-abiding dealing with stability, and single-pointedness of mind and the other penetrative insight emphasizing analysis and discrimination.

Mindfulness: The faculty of mindfulness enables the mind to maintain its attention on a referent object, making it familiar and creating the ability to retain its imprint within the memory for future recollection. It also counteracts forgetfulness.

Negativity: Negativity or non-virtue results in creating a momentum towards a less favorable rebirth within cyclic existence because it arises from the performance of non-virtuous past actions, along with the negative obscurations and their habitual tendencies based on delusion, attachment, and aversion.

Nirvana: It refers to the permanent cessation of all suffering and the dissonant mental states which create suffering, along with all misapprehensions related to the nature of reality. Thus, it is viewed as the anti-thesis of *samsara*.

Omniscience: It indicates the all-knowing pristine cognition of the Buddha. It is understood in terms of a direct and simultaneous perception of the dual aspects of reality, i.e. of the conventional aspects and their ultimate nature.

Refuge: In refuge one entrusts one's spiritual growth and well-being to the three precious jewels of *Buddha*, *Dharma*, and *Sangha*. They are also known as the objects of refuge, and the nature of refuge sought for each of the three is different. In the Buddha, guidance on a correct path to buddhahood is sought, the way one seeks the advice of the doctor; in Dharma, the sacred teachings lead to realizations of the path as the actual medicine; and in *Sangha* (Monastic Community) perfect companionship on the path to buddhahood is sought as the nurse for assistance.

Renunciation: It is defined as a mental attitude to renounce all the causes of miseries such as afflictions and contaminated karmas. It is reflected in the form of not clinging to all worldly attributes such as wealth, fame, position and the thought of a favorable rebirth in a future life. One is also not merely separate from objects of desire but has a mental quality of liberation which is free from even the slightest degree of craving for mundane values.

Sangha: This is the third object of refuge. This generally refers to the community of monks or nuns. Absolute sangha are those who have directly realized emptiness whereas relative sangha are ordained monks and nuns. The Buddhist sangha began with the ordination of a group of five monks to whom the Buddha delivered his first sermon.

Selflessness: It implies lack of inherent existence both in mental and physical phenomena. Besides being an absence of an independently existing self or "I," it embraces all the physical and mental reality. This is equated with emptiness and speaks of the selflessness of person and selflessness of phenomena.

Six Consciousnesses: The six consciousnesses consists of the five sensory and one mental . They are the vision, hearing, smell, taste, touch, and mental consciousness.

Six Perfections: The Bodhisattva clearly needs to practice the six perfections: generosity, ethical discipline, tolerance, joyous effort, concentration, and wisdom. Corresponding results of the practice of the above six perfections are wealth, favorable rebirth, radiance, elegance, peace, and liberation respectively. They also result in longevity, good health, success, and happiness. All the above results arise by the practice of compassion which should be the ground for all the six perfections.

Six Realms of Existence: Six modes of existence are hell, hungry ghost, animal, human, god, and demigod. These are predominantly caused by a particular mental poison hell (anger), of pretas (miserliness), of demigods or asuras (jealousy), and of gods (pride). The karma of beings produces these deluded perceptions.

Suffering: This term is used in a broad sense and includes both sensorial pains and mental experience of pains, i.e. all the unsatisfactory experiences of life in cyclic existence. There are three kinds of suffering: (1) the suffering of suffering, (2) the suffering of change, and (3) the suffering of pervasive conditioning. Suffering also has been identified as the first of the four noble truths. So, one can bring an end to cyclic existence by eliminating suffering through eliminating the ignorance which grasps at inherent existence of phenomena by adopting the entire path of wisdom.

Sutrayana: Here one refers to the Sutra Vehicle or the path to awakening that relies upon the philosophical, ethical and meditative systems as expounded in the Sutra texts. It emphasizes on cultivating three principal practices—renunciation, bodhicitta, and the wisdom to see the final reality of emptiness and dependent origination.

Tantra: The Sanskrit word Tantra means a "continuum" or an "unbroken stream" flowing from the state of ignorance to the state of enlightenment. Tantra has two basic meanings: it is the string of ground, path, and result, and secondly, refers to the literature which expound these continua in the various classes of tantra. Buddhist tantra is grounded on the experience of the teachings of Sutrayana.

Ten Non-Virtuous Actions: These actions are associated with body, speech, and mind. The three physical non-virtues are killing, stealing, and adultery. The four verbal non-virtues are: lying—deceiving others through spoken words or gestures; divisiveness; harsh and senseless speech. The three mental non-virtues are covetousness, harmful intent, and wrong view. Abandoning the ten non-virtuous actions results in freeing one from taking birth in the lower realms.

The Four Reliances: These relate to (1) that one should not rely on the person but the teaching; (2) that one should not rely on the words but the meaning expressed; (3) that one should rely on the definitive meaning and not the provisional meaning; and finally (4) rely on the transcendent wisdom of deep experience and not merely on conceptual knowledge.

The Four Seals: Understanding of the four seals is the ground for the teachings of the Buddha. This is the criterion that distinguishes a school as Buddhist in its acceptance of the following four seals :

All composite phenomena are impermanent

All contaminated things and events are
unsatisfactory.

All phenomena are empty and selfless.

Nirvana is a true peace.

The Noble Eight-fold Path: To overcome suffering
the Noble eightfold path has been suggested. This consists of the right view, right intention, right speech, right
action, right livelihood, right effort, right mindfulness,
and right meditative stabilization.

The Three Jewels: They are (1) the Buddha-Jewel,
which refers to the enlightened teacher, or one's own
future state of enlightenment. This is analogous to an

expert doctor. (2) The Dharma Jewel points to the teachings and realizations that lead to happiness, liberation, and enlightenment. This consists of the third and the fourth noble truths—the truth of freedom from suffering and the truth of the path which leads to this freedom. This is analogous to the medicines which are prescribed by the doctor. Dharma jewel is also known as the ultimate protector. (3) The Sangha-Jewel is the spiritual community of those well established on the path to the freedom from miseries. This is analogous to the nurse who assists the sick people. Just as one recovers fully to enjoy good health with the help of the doctor, medicine and the nurse, with the help of the three jewels, one will be swiftly freed from the fears of samsara to experience lasting happiness and peace.

The Three Kayas: The doctrine of three Kayas or bodies presents the Mahayana understanding of the nature of Buddhahood. The Dharmakaya, or Reality Body, is the ultimate expanse that is the final reality of a Buddha's awakening; it consists of the omniscient mind itself of the Buddha and the ultimate reality of the mind of the Buddha as well. The Sambhogakaya or Enjoyment Body is the form the enlightened Buddha that remains in the perfect realm of existence which is accessible only to the Arya Bodhisattvas. Nirmanakaya, or Emanation Body, is the form of Buddha that is visible to ordinary sentient beings.

Three Levels of Consciousness: These three levels of consciousness deal with the subtlety of consciousness—the gross, the subtle, and very subtle states of mind. The gross consciousness exists in dependence upon the gross physical aggregates and generally can be linked with waking states. The subtle mind is linked with dreaming or intermediate state, and the very subtle consciousness is associated with deep sleep or a continuum of clear light of death.

Three Meanings: This refers to the three kinds of meanings to be achieved: the highest, middle, and the lowest. The highest meaning is to reach full enlightenment, Buddhahood. The middle one is to achieve self-liberation from fears and sufferings of samsara. The lowest meaning is to obtain a peaceful mind within samsara, to solve one's inner problems, and not to be reborn in the lower realms.

Two Truths: All Buddhist schools formulate their ontology within the framework of two truths, the conventional or relative truth, and the ultimate truth. Ultimate truth is defined as the reality as seen by the mind analyzing the ultimate such as the non-dual wisdom mind of the Arya beings. Whereas the conventional truth is experienced through our perceptions as an empirical aspect of reality.

Vajrayana: Vajra has the connotation of inseparability of method and wisdom and also the inseparability of body, speech, and mind. Yana is path. Vajrayana is the path which employs to achieve these two inseparabilities with its unique methods based on the principle of the three paths as cultivated in Sutrayana— renunciation, bodhicitta and the wisdom of emptiness.

Vajrayana is also referred to as Mantrayana and Resultant yana.

Wisdom: It is a mind which correctly understands its object and eliminates doubts pertaining to realities such as impermanence, emptiness of objective existence, and so forth. It mainly implies to all aspects of the path to enlightenment associated with the development of the realization of emptiness.

ABOUT THE AUTHOR

TENZIN GYATSO, HIS HOLINESS THE FOURTEENTH DALAI LAMA, is the spiritual and temporal leader of the Tibetan people. He has written several books on Buddhism and philosophy, and has received many international awards, including the 1989 Nobel Peace Prize in recognition for his advocacy of world peace and inter-religious understanding.

His Holiness describes himself as a simple Buddhist monk. Born on July 6, 1935, to a simple farming family in a small hamlet in Taktsar, Amdo, in northeastern Tibet, he was recognized at the age of two as the reincarnation of the 13th Dalai Lama, Thubten Gyatso.

His Holiness began his monastic education at the age of six. The curriculum consisted of five major and five minor subjects. The major subjects were logic, Tibetan art and culture, Sanskrit, medicine, and Buddhist philosophy. The last was further divided into five categories: *Prajnaparimita*, the perfection of wisdom; *Madhyamika*, the philosophy of the middle Way; *Vinaya*, the canon of monastic discipline; *Abidharma*, metaphysics; and *Pramana*, logic and epistemology. The five minor subjects were poetry, music and drama, astrology, composition and phrasing, and synonyms. At the age of 23, His Holiness sat for his final examination in Lhasa's Jokhang Temple, during the annual Monlam (prayer) Festival in 1959. He passed with honors and was awarded the Geshe Lharampa degree, the highest-level degree, equivalent to a doctorate of Buddhist philosophy.

In 1950 His Holiness was called upon to assume full political power after China's invasion of Tibet in 1949/50. In 1954, he went to Beijing for peace talks with Mao Zedong and other Chinese leaders, including Deng Xiaoping and Chou Enlai. But finally, in 1959, with the brutal suppression of the Tibetan national uprising in Lhasa by Chinese troops, His Holiness was forced to escape into exile. Since then he has been living in Dharamsala, in northern India.

In 1963, His Holiness presented a draft democratic constitution for Tibet that was followed by a number of reforms to democratize the Tibetan administrative setup. In May 1990, the reforms called for by His Holiness were realized as a truly democratic administration in exile for the Tibetan community. The Tibetan Cabinet (Kashag), which until then had been appointed by His Holiness, was dissolved along with the Tenth Assembly of the Tibetan People's Deputies (Tibetan parliament in exile). In the same year, exile Tibetans on the Indian sub-continent and in more than 33 other countries elected 46 members to the expanded Eleventh Tibetan Assembly on a one-person/one-vote basis. The Assembly, in turn, elected the new members of the cabinet. In September 2001, a further major step in democratization was taken when the Tibetan electorate directly elected the Kalon Tripa, the senior-most minister of the Cabinet. The Kalon Tripa then appointed his own cabinet, which had to be approved by the Tibetan Assembly. In Tibet's long history, this was the first time that the Tibetan people elected its political leadership. Since the direct election of the Kalon Tripa, the system of the institution of Gaden Phodrang of the Dalai Lama as both the spiritual and temporal authority ended. Since then, His Holiness has described himself as being semi-retired.

His Holiness the Dalai Lama is a man of peace; the 1989 Nobel Peace Prize was awarded for his advocacy of non-violence in the struggle for the liberation of Tibet. He has consistently advocated policies of non-violence, even in the face of extreme aggression. He has held dialogues with heads of different religions and participated in many events promoting inter-religious harmony and understanding. He is the first Nobel Laureate to be recognized for his concern for the global environment.

Since the mid-1980's, His Holiness has been in dialogue with the scientitific community, mainly in the fields of psychology, neuro-biology, quantum physics, and cosmology. This has led to an historic collaboration between Buddhist monks and world-renowned scientists in trying to help individuals achieve peace of mind, and has introduced modern science into the traditional curriculum of Tibetan monastic institutions, re-established in exile.

His Holiness has travelled to more than 67 countries spanning six continents. He has received over 150 awards, honorary doctorates, and prizes in recognition of his message of peace, non-violence, inter-religious understanding, universal responsibility, and compassion. He is the author of more than 110 books.

ABOUT THE EDITOR

RENUKA SINGH is well-known in the field of Buddhist studies. She has edited *The Dalai Lama's Book of Daily Meditations* and *The Transformed Mind*.

HAMPTON ROADS
PUBLISHING COMPANY

. . . for the evolving human spirit

Hampton Roads Publishing Company publishes books
on a variety of subjects, including spirituality, health,
and other related topics.

For a copy of our latest trade catalog, call (978) 465-0504
or visit our distributor's website at *www.redwheelweiser.*
com. You can also sign up for our newsletter and special
offers by going to *www.redwheelweiser.com/newsletter/*.